Harpers Ferry

TIME REMEMBERED

Harpers Ferry

TIME REMEMBERED

by MARTIN CONWAY

Carabelle Books
P. O. Box 2711
Reston, Virginia 22091

CREDITS

Historical photographs are from the Library of Congress, the National Archives, the West Virginia University and the National Park Service.

Prints and drawings are from the National Park Service and the Library of Congress.

Permission to reproduce paintings were obtained from the Corcoran Gallery of Art, Washington, D. C.; Museum of Fine Arts, Boston; the Walker Art Center, Minneapolis; and the White House Historical Association, Washington, D. C.

In addition to those taken by the author, photographs of the scene today were taken by Christopher Conway and Deborah Mehrkam who also assisted with research. J. Fred Wright and David Martin were responsible for design and layout. Dwight Stinson, Harry Pfanz, Raymond Baker, Robert Nunn and Edwin Bearss—men of the National Park Service—did overall reviews especially as to historical content. Special recognition must go to Thomas and Catherine Halloran for making it all possible. And to my wife, Mary Lou, for her patience and sense of humor when they were most needed.

To this splendid group of people who contributed so much to whatever worth this book may prove, this is dedicated with deepest gratitude, warmth and affection.

Contents

LOUDOUN HEIGHTS

BOLIVAR HEIGHTS

SHENANDOAH RIVER

VIRGINIUS ISLAND

CAMP HILL

ARMORY SITE

POTOMAC RIVER

MARYLAND HEIGHTS

POTOMAC RIVER

ARMORY SITE

JEFFERSON ROCK

ST. PETERS

SHENANDOAH STREET

SHENANDOAH RIVER

III

Foreword

Nowhere on the American scene today is there a place quite like Harpers Ferry. It is a fascinating place whose exciting past and scenic splendor has continually been a source of special interest to both the historian and artist.

This book is a collection of the many lovely prints and engravings of Harpers Ferry created by 19th century artists. Many of these works of art served as illustrations for newspapers of the time.

Among the earliest known works of art of Harpers Ferry is an 1810 sketch of Jefferson Rock with the likeness of Thomas Jefferson standing on it. This was the work of Benjamin Latrobe, one of America's most renown architects and a favorite of Jefferson. The earliest known work is an 1803 print of the general scene by W. Roberts, Esq.

In 1814, Rembrandt Peale—whose portrait of Jefferson is now part of the White House collection—painted a scene of the area that is among the most famous and admired artistic works of Harpers Ferry ever rendered.

During the same period, William H. Bartlett of London sketched two prints of Harpers Ferry for the book, *American Scenery,* published in 1840. These Bartlett prints are now highly popular with collectors of old prints.

TIME REMEMBERED is also a collection of historical photographs—some taken over 120 years ago and many never before seen in print. Photos of the same scene as it appears today are presented beside the historical ones for comparison.

I was unable to locate a photograph taken of Harpers Ferry before 1859. Undoubtedly John Brown's visit was responsible for attracting the first photographer to the town. The earliest photographs, for obvious reasons, were of the armory complex—notably the John Brown Fort and the arsenal—as well as the covered bridge that John Brown and his raiding party used to enter the town.

Much effort was made to photograph today's views from the same location and at the same angle, using approximately the same lens as the original photographer. In many cases, however, the work of nature and subsequent construction made exact duplication impossible. "As close as possible" then became the guiding rule. These photographs were taken in 1979 and 1980.

The photographs are presented in sixteen sections with narratives explaining little-known facts about the early years of Harpers Ferry.

Comparing the past with the present in photographs and prints is a stimulating exercise, especially for one familiar with the area. For someone not familiar with Harpers Ferry, landmarks such as John Brown Fort and the U. S. Armory and names like Lincoln and Jefferson quickly orient the reader to the scene as the photographs lead him through 150 years of history. Harpers Ferry, with its rich legacy and in its stunning setting affords a wealthy opportunity for a study in contrast.

HARPER'S FERRY,

VIRGINIA

Prelude

Across the Shenandoah with Maryland Heights in the background, this scene today is as appealing and unspoiled as depicted in the 1833 painting on the opposite page.

Harpers Ferry 1833 W. J. Bennett
Karolik Collection
Courtesy, Museum of Fine Arts, Boston.

3

VIEW OF HARPER'S FERRY, JEFFERSON CO., VIRGINIA, AND SURROUNDING COUNTRY.—From a Sketch by our Special Artist.

From *Frank Leslie's Illustrated Newspaper*, 1859.

One of America's great sights—Harpers
Ferry from Maryland Heights.

Harpers Ferry in 1859 at the height of its
prosperity and fame.

—and in 1865 at the close of the Civil War.

Along Shenandoah Street next to the Master Armorer's House about the turn of the century.

High Street across from the Stone Steps in 1941. Home cooking was featured at the Jefferson Rock Inn.

Relaxing with a glass of beer on a day in
May. The year was 1941.

Jefferson's Visit

It was October 25, 1783 that Thomas Jefferson visited Harpers Ferry. From a huge rock teetering on the heights behind the town's only tavern (the Harper House), Jefferson was captivated with the view from that point. In his *Notes on the State of Virginia* this is how he expressed his feelings of that moment:

The passage of the Patowmac through the Blue Ridge is perhaps one of the most stupendous scenes in Nature. You stand on a very high point of land. On your right comes up the Shenandoah, having ranged along the foot of the mountain an hundred miles to seek a vent. On your left approaches the Patowmac, in quest of a passage also. In the moment of their junction they rush together against the mountain, rend it asunder, and pass off to the sea. The first glance of this scene hurries our senses into the opinion, that this earth has been created in time, that the mountains were formed first, that the rivers began to flow afterwards, that in this place particularly they have been damned up by the Blue Ridge of mountains, and have formed an ocean which filled the whole valley; that continuing to rise they have at length broken over at this spot, and have torn the mountain down from its summit to its base. The piles of rock on each hand, but particularly on the Shenandoah, the evident marks of their disrupture and avulsion from their beds by the most powerful agents of nature, corroborate the impression. But the distant finishing which nature has given to the picture, is of a very different character. It is a true contrast to the foreground. It is as placid and delightful as that is wild and tremendous. For the mountain being cloven asunder, she presents to your eye, through the cleft, a small catch of smooth blue horizon, at an infinite distance in the plain country, inviting you, as it were, from the riot and tumult roaring around, to pass through the breach and participate of the calm below. . . . This scene is worth a voyage across the Atlantic. Yet here, as in the neighborhood of the Natural Bridge, are people who have passed their lives within half a dozen miles, and have never been to survey these monuments of a war between rivers and mountains, which must have shaken the earth itself to its centre.

The huge slab of rock from where Jefferson viewed that scene was thereafter referred to as Jefferson Rock. Sometime between 1855 and 1860, the Armory Superintendent ordered pillars placed beneath the rock because it was "endangering the lives and properties of the villagers below." The pillars are of Seneca red sandstone, the same material used for the sidewalk in front of the Master Armorer's house on Shenandoah Street.

Rembrandt Peale: Harpers Ferry 1814.
Collection Walker Art Center, Minneapolis.

Earliest known photograph of Jefferson Rock, taken in 1865.

A Place of Special Delight

National Park Service

—and 115 years later. Jefferson Rock was recorded on maps as early as 1803.

An 1810 drawing of Thomas Jefferson by
Benjamin Latrobe, designer of the U. S.
Capitol.

13

Jefferson Rock at the time of the nation's Centennial. Note the ferry line across the Shenandoah River.

By 1885 a toll bridge across the Shenandoah had replaced the ferry.

From Ed Beyer's *Album on Virginia*, 1857.

The view from Jefferson Rock about 1897. Note the scaffolding on the newly-constructed St. Peter's Catholic Church.

17

RICHARDT PAINTING OF HARPERS FERRY, 1858

The view "worthy of a voyage across the
Atlantic" 196 years after seen by Jefferson.

The Harper House

A year before the Declaration of Independence was signed, Robert Harper, the man for whom Harpers Ferry was named, began construction of a new house on land he acquired from Thomas Lord Fairfax. Situated on a ridge above the flood plain and close to the point where the rivers meet, it presented a splendid sight.

Harper died in 1782 never having occupied the house. Having no children, he left his estate to his niece, Sarah Harper Wager.

For the next twenty-one years the Harper House was under lease, serving as the town's only tavern. In October 1783, it was graced by the presence of Thomas Jefferson, who during his visit was so taken with the area's spectacular scenery—that same scenery that had attracted Robert Harper thirty-six years before—that he described it in detail in his *Notes on the State of Virginia*. George Washington also wrote of staying at "The Tavern" during a visit in 1785.

Over the next 152 years, the house was rented to numerous families and underwent drastic renovations. In the latter part of the 19th century it was occupied by Dr. Nicholas Marmion, a prominent Harpers Ferry physician, and his family. Finally it was left to ruin.

Restored in the 1960's by the National Park Service, and with the aid of the local Garden Club Council, it is furnished today to look as it might have during the Civil War.

The Harper House is the oldest building in the town of Harpers Ferry. It is also among the most historic, made so by the mere mention of it in the writings of Thomas Jefferson and George Washington, if not alone by their sojourns there.

As depicted in this 1803 print, the large building in the center is the arsenal. The large structure to the left of the arsenal is the Harper House. This is the oldest known print of Harpers Ferry.

W. Roberts, Esq., 1803

Noted National Park Service historian, Frederick Tilberg, conducts tour in 1955 of the deteriorating scene.

National Park Service

By 1910 the walkway has developed a definite sag.

Public Way in 1898. The main entrance to the Harper House is on the right, with the cellar opening leading down to the kitchen. To the left are springhouses that provided refrigeration for perishable foods.

The walkway today, as in yesterdays, connects the upper porch of the Harper House with the Harper Garden on the slope above.

In 1980 from the Wager House porch. (The Wager House can be seen in lower left corner of the lower photograph.)

Library of Congress

From the Harper House Garden, about 1870.

The Harper House and adjacent dwellings, about 1870, from the stone steps leading up the hillside.

The alley along the restored Harper House as it appears today. The steps lead to the lower level of the house which served as the kitchen.

The Armory and Arsenal

Upon the insistence of George Washington, the Federal government in 1798, established an armory at Harpers Ferry. The availability of water power, the area's safe distance from the nation's capital in time of war, and a belief that the Potomac would be the main artery westward, were reasons that Washington insisted the gun factory be located at Harpers Ferry.

During its 63 years of existence (1798–1861) the armory produced nearly 600,000 flintlock muskets and rifle-muskets, 4000 pistols, a cannon and millions of bayonets and spare parts.

In March 1803, Meriwether Lewis arrived at Harpers Ferry to obtain supplies for his journey that would soon be known as the Lewis and Clark Expedition. In addition to receiving rifles, tomahawks and knives from the armory, Lewis personally supervised the construction of a collapsible iron-framed canoe.

The type of rifle issued to Lewis was the Model 1803, destined to become the most sought-after firearm ever made at Harpers Ferry. Distinguished by its beauty, simplicity, and toughness, and patterned after the famed Kentucky rifle, it became the first standard military rifle. A total of 4,000 were produced between 1804 and 1808.

The armory also turned out the first military pistols made in this country. Considered the most graceful and balanced American military pistols ever made, they were later chosen as the insignia for the U. S. Army's Military Police.

Forty years before John Brown's raid, another man destined to have an impact on the future course of history arrived at Harpers Ferry. His name was John Hall. Commissioned by the government to manufacture breech-loading rifles, Hall in the process developed the system of interchangeable parts, thus making possible the basis for modern industrialism. Although others had pursued the goal of interchangeability—Eli Whitney for example—it was John Hall who actually attained it.

The end to gunmaking at Harpers Ferry came less than a week after the firing on Fort Sumter. Virginia troops seized the armory and began shipping its machinery to Richmond. Although the buildings were used at the close of the war as warehouses for the Union Army, no serious thought was ever again given to re-establishing a gun works at Harpers Ferry.

From Ed Beyer's *Album on Virginia*, 1857.

This early Civil War photograph of the armory is the only known photograph taken of the main entrance looking in at the works. The bell has already been removed from the cupola of the John Brown Fort.

Now covered by a 15-foot-high railroad embankment, there is little to indicate that here once stood one of America's great centers dedicated to the art of gunmaking.

Wartime view of the burned-out armory. The line of wagons in the foreground suggests the time as 1864 when the armory buildings served as a Union quartermaster depot.

This photograph was taken about the same time as the one above. The hillside in the foreground for the most part, is today covered with a heavy growth of trees and underbrush that makes impossible a contrasting shot of the area as it now appears.

From the Hilltop House Hotel—one of the most harmonious combinations of valley, mountains and rivers to be found anywhere.

766 - POTOMAC & R. R. BRIDGE.

The remains of the U. S. Armory, circa 1882

Except for the lone smoke stack, the armory buildings have vanished forever from the scene. Taken about 1890, these pictures were among the last known views of the famous scene before the John Brown Fort was moved and the railroad tunnel constructed through Maryland Heights.

The arsenal, the building on the left where guns produced in the armory were stored, was the immediate objective of John Brown. This rare picture of the arsenal was taken about 1860 near the engine house that John Brown used as a fortress.

THE BURNING OF THE UNITED STATES ARSENAL AT HARPER'S FERRY, 10 P.M. APRIL 18, 1861.—[SKETCHED BY D. H. STROTHER.]

The movement was regarded as a military necessity, and as such executed. To many of us who looked on, the scenes of that night were inexpressibly sad and solemn. The clouds of fire rolled up magnificently from the depths of the romantic gorge, illuminating the confluent rivers and the overhanging cliffs for miles around, each rock and pinnacle associated with the name of some one of our great historic founders. In the martial column revealed by the blaze there stood arrayed, with deadly ball and bayonet, the first-born pride of a hundred hitherto peaceful and happy families. In the town below, between them and their enemy, were neighbors, friends, and fellow-citizens—the enemies themselves our late patented defenders and countrymen.

Brethren, what has forced this fatal necessity upon us?

"As the smoke and vapor of a furnace goeth before the fire, so reviling before blood."   D. H. S.

We also publish a view of FORT McHENRY, at Baltimore. This fort is held by the United States, and in the event of a fight at Baltimore would probably shell the city. It stands at the extremity of a tongue of land near the geographical centre of the city. In the war of 1812 it was bombarded by the British fleet, without success. It was of this bombardment that the famous song "The Star Spangled Banner" was written.

The small cut on the opposite page exhibits the burning of the bridge at Canton by the Baltimore mob. Both of these pictures are from photographs by W. H. Weaver, of Baltimore.

Burning of the U. S. Arsenal 10 p.m. April 18, 1861

From *Harper's Weekly*—1861

During the Civil War, military tents and shebangs (shacks) dominated the scene.

This is the scene as it appeared about 1898. The arsenal is gone; the John Brown Fort has been removed and in its place stands a new monument. The five cast iron markers were placed there by the War Department describing the capture of Harpers Ferry by Confederate forces. They too are gone.

37

Virginius Island

Along the banks of the Shenandoah River adjacent to Harpers Ferry is Virginius Island, a once-thriving industrial community that emerged prior to the Civil War.

Incorporated as a separate town in 1827, Virginius Island boasted a population of about 200 people. Its factories supplied the needs of the townspeople and complemented the work of the armory. Grain was ground, cloth woven, iron cast, lumber cut, and leather tanned in this busy industrial community. Dams, raceways, archways and canals created a network of channeled water power to its factories.

Water, the source of the island's strength and prosperity, was likewise the cause of its decline and ultimate destruction. Floods, beginning with the violent flood of 1870, destroyed the island's homes, factories and waterways.

Today, except for a few visible archeological ruins, nothing remains to remind one of the exciting, thriving community that Virginius Island once was.

VIEW OF THE ISLAND VIRGINIUS, IN THE SHENANDOAH, AT HARPERS FERRY.

TAKEN NEAR JEFFERSON'S ROCK.

1857 Lithograph of Virginius Island.

Mathew Brady's 1865 view of Virginius Island from Jefferson Rock. The building in the left foreground is the U. S. Armory stable. The Herr Flour Mill (roofless structure above center) was destroyed by Confederate saboteurs.

In this circa 1885 photograph, the flour mill ruins still stand while the new Savery Paper Mill dominates the view. Lake Quigley, in the background, was the site of the Hall Rifle Works (see next page).

National Park Service

The Hall Rifle Works ruins after the Civil War. Today no visible evidence remains of these once handsome structures.

Virginius Island inundated by the 1889
flood.

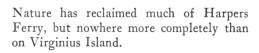

Nature has reclaimed much of Harpers
Ferry, but nowhere more completely than
on Virginius Island.

43

This view of Virginius Island was taken from Jefferson Rock shortly after the Civil War. The devastating flood of 1870 destroyed many of the structures seen here. Note that the Shenandoah appears higher and more turbulent than what is normal at this point. This may well have been the beginning of that devastating flood of 1870.

In this turn of the century scene, the flour mill dominates the brick and stone structures of Virginius Island that survived the 1870 and 1889 floods. But even these were destined to be leveled by floods yet to come.

A lone arch along the Shenandoah River and the Lockwood House on the hill are all that identify this modern scene with the picture above. These photographs were taken from the Pipertown Road that can be seen in the top part of the photo on the opposite page.

The Valley of the Shenandoah,
from Jefferson's Rock.
Harpers Ferry.

The American Centenary, 1876. W. H. Bartlett

Today's remnants of our visible past—these water inlets have been stabilized and are being preserved by the National Park Service.

The three water inlets readily visible in this circa 1882 photo, are among the few structures still standing on Virginius Island.

National Park Service

47

The Bridges

From the town's beginning, the need to cross the waters at the confluence of the Potomac and Shenandoah Rivers has led to the persistent efforts of man to span these rivers. When Robert Harper arrived in 1747, a primitive ferry was already being operated by the first settler, Peter Stephens.

A wooden bridge built across the Potomac in 1824 connected Harpers Ferry, for the first time, directly with the outside world. In 1837, the first railroad bridge was completed and enclosed ten years later with roof and siding to protect the wooden trestles from the elements. This was the covered bridge that John Brown crossed in his October 1859 attack on the town.

During the Civil War the bridge was destroyed nine times, each time to be rebuilt by the tenacious and ingenious men of the Baltimore and Ohio Railroad. This tireless effort ranks among the most persistent engineering accomplishments of the war.

At the close of the war a completely new structure emerged that would remain in service for seventy-two years. Named the Bollman Bridge after its designer, Wendell Bollman, it was at the time among the most famous bridges in the country being constructed wholly of metal. It was destroyed in the 1936 flood.

The trestle bridge that still stands and that initially paralleled the Bollman Bridge was completed in 1893, built in conjunction with the tunnel through Maryland Heights. As the tunnel was dug the bridge served to carry the excavated rock and dirt across the river to Harpers Ferry where it was used to form the railroad embankment. The bridge served as part of the main line of the B & O Railroad until 1931 when the more modern girder bridge was completed and the railroad line relocated to where it is today.

The history of the spanning of the Shenandoah is made less complicated only by the fact that it did not have to provide for trains. By the early 1850's there was a covered toll bridge crossing the Shenandoah about 500 yards from the confluence. When flooding destroyed the bridge, a temporary ferry would operate until the bridge could be rebuilt. In 1882 a new bridge was built across the Shenandoah near the confluence so that one toll collector could collect for both bridges. Although this structure was washed out in the 1889 flood and again in the 1936 flood, its stone piers still stand. It was not until 1949, with the completion of the present bridge further upstream, that the Shenandoah could be crossed without paying toll.

Lithograph by E. Sachse, based on drawing
by Phelps Stokes, ca. 1855.

This photograph taken about 1860 was
most likely used by the artist as the basis
for the print on the opposite page.

Destruction of the railroad bridge by the Rebels (June 14, 1861).

From *Harper's Weekly,* July 6, 1861

A rare close-up of the covered bridge used by John Brown and his raiding party, October 17, 1859.

Completed in 1931, this railroad bridge is
part of the main line of the Baltimore and
Ohio Railroad (Chessie System).

The Bollman Bridge, about 1885, from
Maryland Heights. Note how the bridge is
divided to serve both trains and wagons.

Today, the old bridge pilings stand in ruin, still unwilling to completely yield to the force of the mighty Potomac.

"The Baltimore And Ohio Railroad And Its Branches From The Lakes To The Sea" was the caption that headed this 1871 picture of the Bollman Bridge.

National Park Service

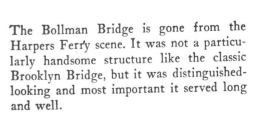

Library of Congress

The Bollman Bridge is gone from the Harpers Ferry scene. It was not a particularly handsome structure like the classic Brooklyn Bridge, but it was distinguished-looking and most important it served long and well.

Woodprint from William C. Bryant's *Picturesque America on the Land We Live In,* 1872.

Workers in 1882 nearing completion of the weak and ill-fated Shenandoah Bridge.

This view was taken about 1885. Notice the completed bridge over the Shenandoah River, destined to be destroyed in the flood four years later.

Except for a single span, the seven year old
bridge has already been swept away in this
scene of the 1889 flood.

This 1931 aerial view shows clearly the evolution of the Harpers Ferry railroad bridges. Note that the newest span is just about completed although the station has yet to be moved.

—and on a beautiful April's day in 1980.

The John Brown Fort

Among America's most famous and historic structures is the John Brown Fort. It is also one of its most interesting. From its moment in history it has been vandalized, victimized, dismantled, and abused—but never forgotten.

Built in 1848 as a fire engine house for the armory, its claim to history was in serving as a stronghold for John Brown and his raiding party.

During the Civil War it was the only building of the armory to escape burning. It was, however, the victim of vandalism by souvenir-hunting troops who continually occupied Harpers Ferry throughout the war. In 1861, for example, the bell hanging from the cupola was removed by a regiment to Marlboro, Massachusetts, where is can still be seen hanging.

In late 1891, the Fort was dismantled and transported to Chicago for display at the Chicago Exposition. Exhibited for ten days, it closed after attracting only eleven people who paid fifty cents each to see it.

About to be converted into a stable, it was rescued by newswoman Mary Kate Fields of Washington, D. C., who in 1895 had it returned to the area. For fourteen years it stood overlooking the Shenandoah River on a farm a few miles from Harpers Ferry.

It was then purchased by Storer College and moved to a site on the campus where it stayed until 1963. At that time the National Park Service—not owning the building's original site—moved it to its present location less than two hundred feet from where it stood seventy-two years earlier.

THE HARPER'S FERRY INSURRECTION.—THE U. S. MARINES STORMING THE ENGINE-HOUSE.—INSURGENTS FIRING THROUGH HOLES IN THE WALL.—FROM A SKETCH MADE ON THE SPOT BY OUR SPECIAL ARTIST.

From *Harper's Weekly* Nov. 1859

63

John Brown's Fort, Harpers Ferry

In 1864, when the burned-out armory was the site of a Union quartermaster depot, the John Brown Fort served as a magazine for gunpowder.

This moment, erected on a 15-foot railroad embankment, marks the site of the John Brown Fort. The base of the monument is about where the Fort's cupola would have been.

As the only building of the armory to escape burning, the John Brown Fort emerged from the Civil War intact but considerably ravaged by souvenir-hunting troops.

The Fort in 1890 with a 10-pounder Parrott rifle in the foreground. Today the gun, mounted in concrete, is displayed in the town's park on Camp Hill.

The John Brown Fort, about 1898, on the Murphy farm where it was located on its return from Chicago.

In 1924 on the campus of Storer College. It was erected there in 1909 on the occasion of the 50th anniversary of the John Brown Raid.

67

68

Storer College students, faculty members and their families on the campus in front of the John Brown Fort for what appears to be an evening choral session. The time was about 1915.

Members of the Colored Women's League before the John Brown Fort on the Murphy Farm. The time was July 1896, during their annual meeting in Washington, D. C.

The Fort in 1891, before being dismantled
and shipped to Chicago.

The John Brown Fort today. During its four moves it was dismantled three times, appearing today smaller and with the guard house on the opposite side from where it was originally.

The War Years

During the American Civil War, Harpers Ferry was the focus of much military activity. Strategically located at the lower end of the Shenandoah Valley, it was intermittently fought over and occupied by one side or the other throughout the four-year struggle.

With the approach of Virginia forces that threatened the town in the earliest phase of the war, the small U. S. Army detachment there was ordered to destroy both the armory and the arsenal. On April 18, 1861 the arsenal—the immediate objective of the John Brown raid a few years before—was set aflame and destroyed with 16,000 arms inside. The armory escaped serious destruction, being saved by local townspeople.

Upon their evacuation of the town two months later, the Confederates in turn set fire to the armory buildings and destroyed the covered bridge over the Potomac.

Two weeks later on June 28, 1861, they returned—their mission this time to destroy the Hall Rifle Works. And if that were not enough, in October Confederate saboteurs entered town and in an act of petty retaliation burned Abraham Herr's four-story flour mill on Virginius Island.

The major military action involving Harpers Ferry occurred in September 1862 just before the Battle of Antietam, when Confederate forces under General Thomas J. "Stonewall" Jackson occupied Maryland and Loudoun Heights and brought the town under siege. Jackson's subsequent attack on the Union lines on Bolivar Heights was met by only token resistance and resulted in the surrender of the 12,500-man Union garrison.

As a result of the war, the town was left battered with most of its buildings in ruins, its major industry—gunmaking—destroyed, and its people scattered, many of whom never returned. While the census of 1870 records no figure for Harpers Ferry, the adjacent town of Bolivar dropped from a population of 1,130 in 1860 to 292 in 1870.

But like every town and city in America ravaged by war, Harpers Ferry would have most certainly recovered, although never again as a leading gun manufacturing center. It was the rampaging waters of the Shenandoah and Potomac Rivers that inevitably marked the decline of Harpers Ferry as a viable center of commerce and industry.

SECESSION BATTERY AT HARPER'S FERRY, ERECTED ON THE HEIGHT OVERLOOKING THE TOWN AND COMMANDING THE RAILROAD BRIDGE, CANAL, &c.—FROM A SKETCH TAKEN WITHIN A FEW DAYS BY OUR SPECIAL ARTIST.—SEE PAGE 35.

Harpers Ferry under Confederate occupation, May, 1861.

From *Frank Leslie's Illustrated Newspaper,* 1861.

Harpers Ferry early in the Civil War.

Imp. Ch. Chardon aîné.   Paris

Outhwaite sc

HARPER'S FERRY

Harpers Ferry, 1861.

75

This replacement span, completed in August 1862, was in use only a month when Gen. Thomas Jackson ordered it destroyed when his Confederate troops evacuated the town.

This 1862 photo from the Mathew Brady collection shows the Union pontoon bridge under construction. It was during the night of September 14, 1862 that 2,500 Union cavalry escaped capture by crossing this pontoon bridge even though both heights overlooking the bridge were in Confederate hands.

During the Gettysburg Campaign, a small force of Confederates laid flooring across the railroad bridge at Harpers Ferry. This remarkable photo, taken on July 5, 1863, shows the flooring on fire, a measure taken by Union forces. Lee's main army was at that moment beginning their long, sad retreat from Gettysburg.

After a devastating war and violent periodic flooding, the
piers that supported those historic bridges still defiantly
stand 143 years after they were built.

79

This print was made for members of the 5th New York Heavy Artillery to commemorate the special relationship that the regiment had with Harpers Ferry. During the war, the regiment served in Harpers Ferry longer than any other Union outfit. And it was from Harpers Ferry on July 19, 1865—three months after Appomattox—that the entire complement was honorably discharged and mustered out of Federal service. (See page 88 for picture of encampment.)

On Camp Hill today, there is no visible evidence of these fortifications. The fortifications began on the grounds of what is now known as Mather Training Center. Making allowances for Wirth Hall, the line followed the high ground along Jackson Street to the heights over-looking the Potomac.

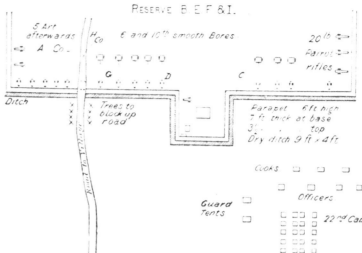

PLAN OF WORKS AT HARPERS FERRY. JULY 19.1862.

RESERVE B. E. F. &I.

This good-looking military unit is Company A, 22nd New York militia pictured during the summer of 1862. The Lutheran Church on Washington Street is in the background; the building on the right is the public school.

On June 28, 1861 Confederate forces returned to Harpers Ferry. After destroying the Hall Rifle Works on Virginius Island, they burned the covered bridge over the Shenandoah, pushed an engine into the Potomac, and left.

LOCOMOTIVE AND TENDER THROWN FROM THE RAILWAY BRIDGE AT HARPER'S FERRY BY THE REBELS.

From *Harpers Weekly—July 20, 1861*

Shenandoah suspension bridge in ruins. Loudoun Heights is in the background.

From *Harpers Weekly—1864*

Union troops on the move through town, October 1862.

THE MAIN STREET, HARPER'S FERRY, VA.—ZOUAVES ON MULES—CONTRABANDS HAULING GUNS—OFFICERS LOUNGING, &C., OCTOBER 16.—SKETCHED BY OUR SPECIAL ARTIST, MR. EDWIN FORBES

From *Frank Leslie's Illustrated Newspaper* —1862

General N. P. Banks' troops crossing the Potomac in the winter of 1862.

WAR IN VIRGINIA—GENERAL BANKS'S DIVISION OF THE ARMY OF THE POTOMAC CROSSING THE POTOMAC RIVER, AT HARPER'S FERRY, FEBRUARY 26TH.—FROM A SKETCH BY OUR SPECIAL ARTIST MR. C. S. HALL.

From *Harpers Weekly*—1862

83

Maryland Heights: Siege of Harpers Ferry, 1863.
William MacLeod
The Corcoran Gallery of Art—
Gift of Genevieve Plummer

From Maryland Heights looking up the Potomac.

Lincoln's Visit

It was October 1, 1862 when President Abraham Lincoln visited Harpers Ferry.

Arriving by train, the President was taken to General Edwin V. Sumner's headquarters (now Mather Training Center) where he met briefly with General George B. McClellan. Afterwards they all traveled to Bolivar Heights to review the fighting men of the tough Union II Corps.

The President then went into town to inspect the railroad bridge under repair and to see the engine house that John Brown and his men had used as a fort three years earlier. Lincoln then returned to Sumner's headquarters where he spent the night.

The next morning after inspecting fortifications and troops on Loudoun and Maryland Heights, President Lincoln left for Sharpsburg.

President Abraham Lincoln and General George McClellan at Antietam the day after Lincoln visited Harpers Ferry

VIEW OF HARPER'S FERRY.

From Horace Greeley's *The American Conflict*, 1865. (1861 view)

THE FEDERAL CAMP ON BOLIVAR HEIGHTS, 1862

88

An 1862 encampment of the 5th New York Heavy Artillery in front of the Commanding General's Headquarters. Built in 1847 as the residence for the Armory Superintendent, the building was situated on commanding heights surrounded by spacious grounds. It was here that President Abraham Lincoln spent the night of October 1, 1862.

Wirth Hall, named to honor former National Park Service Director Conrad Wirth, is the main building of Mather Training Center. The left wing is the original structure (see opposite page); the center section with cupola and the right wing, that gave overall balance to the structure, were constructed by Storer College in 1881. It was rebuilt in 1928 after a fire greatly damaged it the year before.

Storer College

In 1867 Storer College was founded through the co-operative efforts of the Freewill Baptist Church, the Freedman's Bureau, and John Storer, a wealthy Maine merchant. It was one of the first colleges established after the Civil War to educate the newly freed blacks.

Makeshift classrooms were initially set up in the Lockwood House, one of the four former armory residences donated by the Government to the school. These buildings became the nucleus of the new college. As more funds were contributed, the college expanded its facilities to make room for a growing student body. By 1889, it could claim an enrollment of 273 students.

In August 1906, the second conference of the Niagara Movement—forerunner of the National Association for the Advancement of Colored People—met at Storer. Under the distinguished historian and sociologist, W. E. B. Du Bois, the Niagara Movement was the first national organization that aggressively and unconditionally demanded the same rights for their people as enjoyed by white America.

In 1955 financial difficulties compelled Storer College to close. But the spirit of its tradition and success survives. Today its buildings and campus serve as a National Park Service training center in furthering America's great contribution to world culture—the national park idea.

THE WAR IN UPPER VIRGINIA—GEN. SHERIDAN'S HEADQUARTERS AT HARPER'S FERRY.—FROM A SKETCH BY OUR SPECIAL ARTIST, J. E. TAYLOR.

Built in 1847 as quarters for the Armory Paymaster, the Lockwood House during the Civil War served as headquarters for Generals Henry H. Lockwood and Philip H. Sheridan. After the war the building became the birthplace of Storer College.

National Park Service

Storer College as it appeared about 1905. The men's dormitory, the building on the left, was destroyed by fire in 1909.

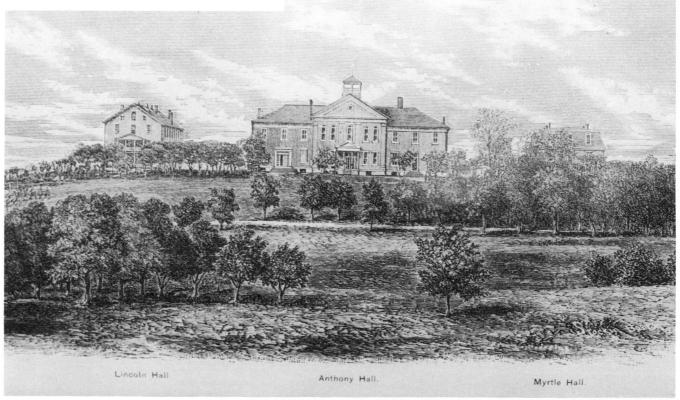

Storer College, 1889 from the college catalogue

Lincoln Hall.   Anthony Hall.   Myrtle Hall.

—and from the opposite direction taken at about the same time. The Lutheran Church is on the left—see page 81 for an earlier view.

National Park Service

Storer College Campus, about 1924.

95

National Archives   An advertisement after the Civil War announcing that things on the railroad were nearly back to normal.

Transportation

Throughout most of the 19th century, Harpers Ferry was a thriving center of trade and commerce. Roadways, railroads, ferry lines and canals all played an important role in shaping the history and culture of the town. Indeed, the town's very name is derived from an early settler, Robert Harper, and the ferry he operated.

During the first decade of the 19th century the Potowmack Company—whose first president was George Washington—constructed a canal to "by-pass the Shenandoah falls at Mr. Harper's Ferry." This is the same canal one initially sees upon entering Harpers Ferry along Shenandoah Street.

The United States Armory Canal along the Potomac was the area's first canal and the only one still operating today, providing the community with electrical power.

In the early 1830's, the Baltimore and Ohio Railroad and the Chesapeake and Ohio Canal raced to see which could first reach Harper's Ferry and take advantage of the lucrative opportunities that lay beyond. The C & O Canal reached Harpers Ferry in 1833, about one year before the B & O Railroad's arrival.

The canals are of another age and the ferry has long ago vanished from the scene. But the railroad and roadways remain, serving the town in ways that those of that distant age could never have dreamed.

HARPER'S FERRY—THE SCENE OF THE LATE INSURRECTION.

From *Harpers Weekly*, 1859

Across the Potomac from Harpers Ferry is Lock 33 of the Chesapeake and Ohio Canal. Pictured here in 1876, it was one of the busiest points along the 184 mile waterway.

The remains of Lock 33 today are part of
the Chesapeake and Ohio Canal National
Historical Park.

An 1876 view of the ferry across the Shenandoah River. (Also refer to page 14.)

The sight of raft trips down the Shenandoah has replaced the ferry that long ago vanished from the scene.

A 1910 scene at the Harpers Railroad Depot.

The track on the right, once the main line of the Baltimore and Ohio Railroad, is now a little used siding. The
John Brown Fort monument is in the center of the picture.

Built in 1894, this railroad station served the town until 1931 when the main line of the railroad was relocated and the station moved to its present location.

Without its commanding tower, the relocated railroad
station bears little resemblance to the distinguished and
proud structure it once was.

The Streets

SHENANDOAH STREET

Named for the river it parallels, Shenandoah Street remains Harpers Ferry's most famous and scenic roadway. Due to the steepness of High Street, Shenandoah Street was the road used by horse-drawn vehicles to Charles Town and points west. And it was along this road that John Brown, under escort, was taken to Charles Town to be tried.

HIGH STREET

High Street is the direct route to Bolivar and the Camp Hill section of Harpers Ferry at which point it becomes Washington Street. As floods discouraged development in the lower part of the town, an increasing number of shops and dwellings were relocated along the steep banks of the street. Today High Street and its narrow sidewalks cater to visitors attracted to the legacy and scenery of the area.

GENERAL VIEW OF HARPER'S FERRY, SHOWING THE BRIDGE, ARMORY, ADJACENT HILLS, ETC.—[SEE PAGE 712.]

From *Harpers Weekly*, 1859.

From *Gleason's Pictorial*, 1854.

Shenandoah Street, about 1880.

—and as a national historical park, 100 years later.

—and 50 years later.

A 1930 scene at the corner of High and Shenandoah Streets.

Harpers Ferry as it appeared in 1932 during the Great Depression.

In this park scene, the life and sparkle and excitement of a living community is gone, perhaps forever. Imaginative adaptive use however, of many of these historic structures by private firms and individuals, might well restore its vigor, charm and sense of excitement; while at the same time keeping something of that tough, honest and unpretentious remnant of a 19th century working town.

111

MANUFACTURER OF TINWARE AND DEALER IN STOVES & HARDWARE.

ONERY.

High Street in 1886. The Stone Steps to Jefferson Rock can be seen on the left.

These pictures were taken from the same spot—although
at different angles—probably on the same day but at least
an hour apart judging from the building shadows.

National Park Service

HIGH STREET, HARPER'S FERRY, W. VA.

At the foot of High Street where it meets
Shenandoah Street, about 1900.

The streets of Harpers Ferry have always been trodded upon by colorful characters that lent certain dash and controversy to its lusty atmosphere. That tradition continues by men with names the likes of Nash, Brawley, Miller, Smallwood and Kilham. And although Harpers Ferry is a rugged town, its fabric is fragile. That fabric is composed of such things as use, scale, history, art and character. It is a balance that is tenuous at best and tenable only through constant care.

A detachment of Doughboys marches down High Street during World War I.

This 1885 view of High Street is often referred to as the "Cow Picture." The row of buildings behind the man standing on the ledge, was destroyed by fire at the turn of century.

OPEN
DAILY
ALL YEAR

117

Lovely Shenandoah Street on a spring day in the 1880's.
The wooden bridge to Virginius Island was destroyed in the flood of 1889.

The Randolph Bridge, dedicated in 1974 to U. S. Senator Jennings Randolph of West Virginia, is an exact reconstruction of the original. It was Sen. Randolph who in 1944 introduced legislation establishing Harpers Ferry as a national historical park.

119

The Churches

The people who settled Harpers Ferry brought with them their religious faiths. Until the 1820's and 30's when they began constructing their churches on land donated by the government, congregations met in armory buildings.

The first church, the Free Church, used by many faiths was completed in 1827. In 1845 it was destroyed by fire. It stood on the hillside where the Episcopal Church ruins can be seen today.

Since 1833 St. Peter's Roman Catholic Church has dominated the town's landscape. Situated on a commanding heights above the town the structure presents an impressive sight. Constructed on land donated by Robert Harper, the original was brick with a false front. The present stone structure was built in 1896.

It is alleged that during the Civil War Father Costello, pastor of St. Peter's, regularly displayed the Union Jack as a means of protecting the church. He reasoned that both armies would refrain from inciting an international incident by intruding or firing on a site flying the flag of a neutral country. It apparently worked, since the church escaped the war undamaged. Today it remains active with Mass offered each Sunday at 10:00 a. m.

Nearby stood St. John's Episcopal Church, built on the same site as the earlier Free Church. It was completed in 1852 with money for its construction raised by holding church fairs. During the Civil War the church served as barracks for Confederate artillerymen. After the war only the walls and roof of the fieldstone building with concrete facing remained. The church was rebuilt in 1882, but was sold in 1895 because of declining membership. Later a new church was built in the upper portion of the town.

The only church located in the lower section of the town was the Presbyterian Church along Shenandoah Street. The one and a half story brick structure was completed in 1843. Although damaged by Federal troops, it was still standing in 1913, but with declining membership was sold.

Besides St. Peter's the only other church which remained active after the war and into recent years is the Lutheran Church located on Camp Hill. The church was completed in 1851 and has been altered very little from its original appearance. Although services were temporarily halted during the war, it is still in use today.

National Park Service

The Presbyterian Church on Shenandoah Street as it appeared shortly after the Civil War. Note the people standing on Jefferson Rock.

HARPER'S FERRY, VIRGINIA, FROM JEFFERSON ROCK.

From *Gleason's Pictorial,* 1854.

St. John's Episcopal Church as it appeared
after the Civil War.

St. John's about 1885, just after it was rebuilt. In the background is the new Shenandoah River Bridge.

St. John's Episcopal Church today is an impressive ruin along the trail to Jefferson Rock.

St. Peter's Roman Catholic Church as it
appeared after the Civil War.

—and today, after being rebuilt 84 years
ago.

Pictured here in 1865 are the famous Stone Steps that were carved out of a rock formation by the early townspeople.

"The Stone Steps, anciently carved in virgin rock
A sweet worn town with old world air
A street that climbs on a stone-laid stair
To fableland and green plateau
With the Shenandoah's song below"
Unknown

Equipped today with hand rails, the Stone Steps provide access to the Harper House, St. Peter's Church, and Jefferson Rock.

125

The churches of St. Peter's and St. John's as they appear in this photo taken about 1888 by the noted Gettysburg photographer, William Tipton.

Of the buildings that survive, the churches underwent the most dramatic changes; St. Peter's is rebuilt, while St. John's stands in ruin amidst the trees.

THE CIVIL WAR IN AMERICA : HARPER'S FERRY, VIRGINIA.

From *London Illustrated News,* 1861.

From the Heights

MARYLAND HEIGHTS

Looming over 1000 feet high, Maryland Heights affords the most extraordinary view of the town and the rivers that frame it. During Robert Harper's time many Highlanders settled atop these heights bringing with them their love and skill for gardening and shepherding. It was then that the area was famous for its fine fruits and vegetables.

In September 1862 Confederate forces, in a spirited attack, drove Union troops off these heights thereby insuring the eventual surrender of the town.

On the summit are the remnants of the Union stronghold built in 1864. It is worthy of a visit and the vigorous climb it takes to reach it.

LOUDOUN HEIGHTS

Along the crest of Loudoun Heights—the boundary between Virginia and West Virginia—is the famed Appalachian Trail. Running parallel at its base is the swift-flowing Shenandoah River. Together they provide a rich diversity of recreational opportunities amid historic settings and lovely scenery.

BOLIVAR HEIGHTS

It was on Bolivar Heights on September 15, 1862, that 12,500 Union troops, after offering little or no resistance, surrendered to the Confederate forces of General "Stonewall" Jackson. And it was on Bolivar Heights a few weeks later that the fighting men of the tough Union II Corps marched in review before General George B. McClellan and President Abraham Lincoln. Still evident today along the ridge are Civil War period earthworks.

An Amtrak train crossing the Potomac at Harpers Ferry.

W. H. Bartlett, *American Scenery*, 1839.

From Maryland Heights in 1896.

From all sides, nature attempts to reclaim the site.

From *Frank Leslie's Illustrated Newspaper*, 1862.

Flying low over Loudoun Heights provides
a unique view of Maryland Heights.

From Loudoun Heights in 1895. The
building in the foreground with arches is
the old marketplace.

—and in the summer of 1979.

This view from Loudoun Heights was most likely taken a short time before the 1895 view on page 134.

Most of the post-Civil War structures are
gone from the scene, demolished when the
lower town became a national park.

Contemplating the Harpers Ferry scene in 1932 from Loudoun Heights. Note the new spans on the Bollman Bridge, replacements of the ones destroyed during the 1924 flood.

Hiking along the Appalachian Trail on Loudoun Heights. Harpers Ferry is midpoint along the 3000 mile trail and the location of the Appalachian Trail Conference.

—and in 1979 looking up the Potomac from the Appalachian Trail. The Shenandoah is on the left.

139

Unknown

This 1826 painting was the basis for the 1857
Currier and Ives lithograph (opposite).

Currier and Ives, 1857.

The Waters

Harpers Ferry, like the mighty Grand Canyon of the Colorado, owes its inspiring beauty to the power of water. Millions of years ago as the mountains rose from the flat land, the waters of what are now the Potomac River served as a carving knife resisting the upheaval of the land. (This is contrary to Thomas Jefferson's theory; see his *Notes on the State of Virginia,* page 10.)

From its creation to its demise, the history of Harpers Ferry is based on water power. Gun factories were established due to the abundant supply of water —water to turn wheels that formed metal and wood into guns. And it was because of those guns that John Brown came to Harpers Ferry.

And it was water power out of control that caused Harpers Ferry's ultimate decline. Ironically these floods were responsible for preserving the town as one of the finest examples of 19th century America left today.

This is how it happened. During its initial effort to recover from the Civil War, Harpers Ferry in 1870 was dealt a devastating blow. The surging waters of the Shenandoah destroyed seventy buildings, leveled Virginius Island and claimed forty-two lives including three entire families of over twenty people. This and subsequent floods lay waste the economy of the town.

Consequently, building modifications and improvements were discouraged, leaving intact a 19th century town that affords a splendid example of our visible past. Out of this emerged a national park to be preserved for all time to come by a sensitive people aware of the priceless legacy of Harpers Ferry.

HARPER'S FERRY.

The 1870 flood was the greatest natural disaster that Harpers Ferry has ever experienced. What made it so devastating was that only the Shenandoah flooded its banks. Had the Potomac been at flood stage at the same time—as in the case of subsequent floods—it would have served to restrict the force of the swift-flowing Shenandoah.

Harpers Weekly, 1870.

143

The aftermath of the 1889 flood looking south on Shenandoah Street near the intersection of High Street.

Shenandoah Street taken from the railroad
embankment at the height of the 1924 flood.

National Park Service

The 1936 flood as it begins to recede. Compare the water level with that of the 1924 flood.

During the 20th century, four major floods
have thus far innundated the town.

The last close-up of the magnificent Bollman Bridge as it yields to the relentless
waters of the Potomac during the flood of
1936.

The rampaging Potomac during the flood
of 1936. Shortly after this photo was taken,
the 72 year old Bollman Bridge on the
right collapsed.

Harpers Ferry, flanked by Maryland Heights on the right, as it appears looking upstream on the Potomac.

From *The History and Topography of the
United States of America,* 1852.

Since 1955

With the dawn of 20th century America and the hope and vision that it brought, Harpers Ferry was struggling to survive. War and floods had reduced the place to an unwanted and nearly forgotten shadow of its former self.

Amid decay and seemingly with no hope of recovery, there were a few far-sighted people—most notably Henry McDonald, President of Storer College—who insisted that Harpers Ferry should be preserved for its cultural importance to the nation.

Congress finally agreed and enacted legislation in 1944, establishing Harpers Ferry as a National Monument. In 1955, after taking ten years to acquire the authorized land, the State of West Virginia donated 619 acres to the Federal government. And in 1960, the state of Maryland donated Maryland Heights, consisting of 763 acres.

Today, Harpers Ferry National Historical Park includes about one-third of the town, as well as land on Bolivar Heights, Loudoun Heights and Maryland Heights. Nearly a million people visit the Park each year.

Under the National Park Service, the Park is managed for the benefit and enjoyment of people everywhere, to be preserved for all time to come for those of us today and for generations yet unborn.

HARPER'S FERRY.

Picturesque B & O, 1883.

By 1955, Harpers Ferry streets were mean tokens of neglect from the excitement and activity that once stirred them. But even amid a state of widespread decay, for those with sensitive insight there were sudden and lovely surprises.

Devastated by abuse and neglect, Harpers Ferry in 1955, is at last entrusted to the care of the National Park Service.

Due primarily to the special interest of U. S. Senator Robert C. Byrd of West Virginia, buildings throughout the Park are being restored so that those of us today, and especially generations yet unborn, can enjoy and appreciate this unique place on the American landscape and in American history.

Aerial views taken in 1955 at the time Harpers Ferry became a unit of the National Park System.

—from higher up in 1980.

Looking Back . . . and Farewell

This limited edition of
HARPERS FERRY — time remembered
is set in 11 on 12 point Caslon type,
printed by Kingsport Press on
60# Monadnock-Dulcet paper
1981